Which came first, the chicken or the egg? Historians were faced with a similar question when trying to identify the exact origin of the railway. It's thought that the Greeks and Romans developed grooved stone waggonways, although whether these were deliberately cut or simply worn into the road surface is difficult to say.

One thing we can be sure of is the reason for its invention. Quite simply, it made life easier. Moving heavy loads before the railway would have been exhausting work. Roads were muddy, rough and difficult to maintain – not ideal by any stretch of the imagination. Pushing or pulling trucks along smooth rails on the other hand was far more appealing, particularly when the tracks guided the wagons too.

Mining

It was in European mines during the fifteenth century where railways really caught on. Mine trucks were fitted with a hanging metal pin which slotted in between two wooden planks, thus guiding them along – a replica of such a wagon is in the Museum.

These carts were known as 'dogs' by the miners because of the noise they made. Although, as they had to use muscle power to push them around all day, they no doubt received less flattering names as well. In Britain, similar trucks were being used in the Lake District.

Around 1600 in Nottingham, a railway was being built to carry coal to the city and the River Trent. Soon waggonways, as they came to be known, were to be found in the Severn Valley and Tyneside and from these two centres the idea spread throughout Britain and back into Europe.

Demand

Railways were still being made of wood at the end of the eighteenth century, but things were changing. Demand for new tracks was growing, as the owners of canals (the motorways of the time) continually requested connecting lines into the canal network. At the same time, ever-increasing industrialisation meant that iron was becoming relatively cheap. And it wasn't long before stronger and more hard-wearing cast-iron rails started to appear, enabling the railways to carry heavier loads.

Horse power

Outside the mines, horses had long taken over from man as the main source of propulsion. Interestingly, to this day the railway gauge (the distance between the rails) remains at 4 ft 8½ ins – the width required to allow a horse to walk in between the rails.

Horse power was expensive and as demand rose, so too did the need for them to travel further. The introduction of the 'Dandy Cart' was one answer. By giving the horse a free ride downhill, it could travel up to 240 miles a week. You can see such a cart, once owned by the Stockton & Darlington Railway, in the Museum's collection.

Despite these developments, the search continued for a mechanical device that could do better. And so fixed steam engines – like the *Weatherhill* and the *Leicester & Swannington* engines in the Museum's Great Hall – began pulling trains at the end of a cable. But by 1804, the first steam locomotive rolled on to the tracks. Even so, in 1825 when the first scheduled passenger service was introduced on the Stockton & Darlington Railway, horses were the motive power – locomotives hauled only the slower, heavier coal trains.

In fact, horses continued to be used for some time, until that is, an engineer called Stephenson had a brainwave. But that's another story.

Rocket
Racing ahead of her time

You need to do something pretty special to be commemorated on an English banknote and *Rocket* was no exception.

It all started in 1803 when Richard Trevithick invented the first steam locomotive. It was a great leap forward, but unfortunately the locomotive itself didn't so much leap forward as crawl, but at least it worked. In the years that followed over 50 other engines were built to a similar design.

The jobs they could perform however were limited because of three problems: they used too much coal, they were painfully slow, and they were unreliable.

The Challenge

So in 1829 when the first inter-city line was being built – from Liverpool to Manchester – the directors of the company put out a challenge.

They offered a purse of £500 to anyone able to better the existing locomotives.

The requirements: to pull three times its own weight along 1¾ miles of track forty times – the equivalent of Liverpool to Manchester and back – at an average speed of 10 mph.

The thought of winning such a sum was enough to excite every locomotive builder in the land; none more so than George Stephenson and his son Robert.

Stephenson's breakthrough

The sectioned replica of *Rocket* in the Museum shows the three innovations the Stephensons brought together in their engine. They first made the boiler more effective by using a mass of small tubes – not a single large one – to heat the water. They then improved upon the fire itself. Sending the exhaust steam from the cylinders up the chimney created a vacuum, which drew air through the fire, making it burn more fiercely

and in the process, producing the familiar 'chuff'. Thirdly, they simplified the connecting rods between cylinders and wheels to improve the driving mechanism and reduce the chance of a breakdown.

The finished engine was to revolutionise the future of steam locomotives and the railway. They called it '*Rocket*'.

So to the big day – the Rainhill Trials as they were known. For those who entered, the pressure was intense. Not only had they to demonstrate their machines in front of the railway directors, but in addition, thousands of spectators had turned out.

Triumphant

When Stephenson's turn came, he opened up *Rocket* and completed the course of 70 miles at an average speed of 13 mph.

All other entrants were forced to withdraw after breaking down. Although at one time, two machines, *Novelty* and *Sanspareil*, looked as though they might challenge *Rocket* for the prize, in the end, they too had to quit.

Rocket was triumphant and the Stephensons were to receive fame and fortune far greater than the original prize money. And that wasn't all. It would appear that George had become quite popular with the ladies. One year after the Rainhill Trials, following a ride on *Rocket*, a young actress named Fanny Kemble described him as "a master" that she was "horribly in love with".

Sadly for *Rocket*, her grand prize for winning turned out to be a few years' service on the Liverpool & Manchester Railway before being sold to work as a freight engine. She was, after all, only a prototype and was soon superseded by more refined production models. Nevertheless, her basic design principles were ground-breaking and were included in all steam locomotive designs thereafter. Her place in history was secure.

In 1862 she was donated to the Patent Office Museum and is now on display in the Science Museum in London. A working replica can be found at the National Railway Museum, a shining example of the pioneering days of steam.

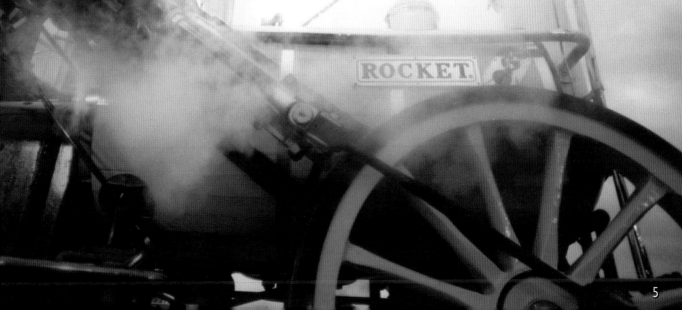

BLOOD
SWEAT
& BEERS

It didn't take long for people to jump on the bandwagon following the success of *Rocket* and the Liverpool & Manchester Railway.

Throughout Britain, people were clamouring for new lines: level-headed businessmen keen to move their goods quickly, local politicians anxious to see that their town didn't end up as a backwater and inevitably, speculators ready to seize the opportunity to 'get rich, quick'. People were going train crazy. In the late 1830s and mid 1840s, money was being thrown at the railway to such an extent that the term 'Railway Mania' was born.

Perhaps the most famous of these speculators was George Hudson of York, 'The Railway King' as he was crowned.

Hudson's investment

He became involved in so many schemes with so many companies that at one time he co-owned 1,000 miles of track. Sadly, greed got the better of Mr Hudson who eventually fell into disrepute by his misuse of shareholders' capital. A bust of him is on display in the Balcony Galleries.

In 1849, his fame was captured in a decidedly double-edged poem by Gladstone that read:

"How many thousands that counted their gains
Were miniature Hudsons, excepting their brains!
Who, I ask, were the Shareholders, greedy of gold
That bought when he bought and sold when he sold?"

Such was the railway boom, that within 20 years of the Rainhill Trials, around 5,000 miles of track criss-crossed the country. Neither the Romans with their roads and civic buildings nor the canals with their locks and aqueducts had made such an impact on the British countryside.

Engineers such as George and Robert Stephenson, Isambard Kingdom Brunel and Joseph Locke designed thousands of miles of railway lines and had never been so busy. Some of the surveying equipment used in planning these tracks is on display in the Museum. Numerous problems faced these engineers, but Robert Stephenson summed up their spirit when writing in 1848 of his Conway Bridge:

"The difficulty we are contending with is much greater than I anticipated, but I will never give up."

The bridge was completed and opened later that year.

Railway contractors like Thomas Brassey and Samuel Peto worked for Locke and the Stephensons, employing thousands of construction workers to do the arduous task of digging and blasting through soil and rock, making cuttings and tunnels and building countless bridges, embankments and viaducts.

The workers

Skilled labourers could now demand twice the wage of an agricultural worker. These men (called 'navvies' like their predecessors who built the navigation canals) were now earning enough money to splash out on life's little luxuries, like steak, whisky and plush waistcoats.

But their new-found wealth was resented by some, who described them as "infidels, hard-drinkers, stout fighters, lovers of dogs and pigeons and other men's orchards and poultry yards".

Still, come boom or bust, hard work and harder drinking, the railways were fast becoming part of the landscape. Charles Dickens wrote in 'Dombey and Son':

"The neighbourhood which had hesitated to acknowledge the railroads in its straggling days.....now boasted of its powerful and prosperous relation."

It was true; the railway was here to stay.

Harrow Station, 8 October 1952.

An express train on its way to Euston was running over 30 minutes late, so as usual the station's signalman let a local commuter train, also travelling to London, run in front. The morning was much the same as any other.

The commuter train rolled into the station just before 08.20 to receive its passengers. Rush hour crowds soon filled many of the carriages, forcing the train's guard to open the guard's van at the rear and allow passengers to stand inside.

Missed signals

Watching them board, he became aware of a train entering the station. It was the delayed express; and it was on the same track. Its driver had missed two stop signals and only started to slow down when he saw the standing commuter train in front of him. But applying the brakes then, was little more than procedure.

The locomotive – one of the fastest in the country – ploughed into the waiting commuter train with such violence that its last three carriages were crushed to the size of one. The express train jumped the rails, landing on another track. Debris flew everywhere. People walking on a footbridge over the track fell to their death as mangled carriages slammed into the supporting girders.

Danger signals immediately lit up in a desperate attempt to stop more trains entering the station. But it was too late. Another express, travelling north, was already on its way in at 60 mph. Pulled by two locomotives, the train ran straight into the path of the derailed express.

Horrified commuters ran for their lives once again, as the force of the impact sent the two locomotives flying across the platform, finally coming to rest on the other side.

Carnage

As the dust settled, the scale of the disaster became evident. Wreckage was spread across an immense area. In the centre, carriages were piled on top of each other in a mass of twisted metal and shattered wood. It was to be Britain's worst peacetime rail disaster;

112 people lost their lives and in a bizarre twist of fate, 64 of them were railway employees on their way to work.

Important lessons were learnt that day.

Safety measures

Safety has always been of the utmost importance. Soon after the railway's introduction, it was realised that some form of signalling was required.

To begin with, the job fell to policemen who warned oncoming trains of hazards by using hand signals, but they were soon replaced with actual fixed signals beside the track. Trains would simply follow each other after a minimum time period had elapsed, but this system had a serious flaw. It didn't allow for one train travelling faster than expected; should the locomotive in front break down, the following one only found out shortly before its inevitable collision. Improvements were needed.

The solution was block-signalling. This meant that tracks were divided into sections called 'blocks'.

A train could not enter a 'block' until the previous one had left it. Signals for this soon developed into grouped systems operated from raised signal boxes – the extra height giving signalmen a better view of the lines on either side. You can see exactly how these work in 'The Working Railway' gallery and even have a go at it yourself. The electric telegraph helped to pass messages regarding whether the line was clear.

Encouraged from time to time by legislation, the railways steadily updated their signalling. In 1894 electrically-operated train detection devices (track circuits) were introduced. With the arrival of the electric age, mechanical systems and semaphore signals, with their distinctive red and yellow arms, have slowly given way to coloured lights controlled from a smaller number of signalling centres.

Hi-tech

Today the Integrated Electronic Control Centre (IECC) brings computer programming to signalling. Trains are dealt with according to a timetable in

the impact of DISASTERS

the computer's memory, although signallers can override it should they need to. York's IECC is replicated in real time in 'The Working Railway' and you can watch the progress of trains through York on the East Coast Main Line.

Railway accidents in which lives are lost are always followed by an enquiry. After the tragic crash at Harrow, it was recommended that an Automatic Warning System be fitted inside locomotive cabs to alert drivers should they pass a red signal and, if still no action is taken, to apply the brakes automatically.

The lessons learnt from past disasters, such as Harrow and the earlier 1905 accident at County Durham which is pictured below, have led to the modern railway becoming one of the safest forms of transportation.

new trains

new tracks new business

Just as the railway looked like running out of surprises, someone decided to build a track under the sea!

However, it could so easily have been a different story. The French and British Governments received a number of suggestions for the cross channel link, varying from a combined bridge and submerged tube system to a motorway suspension bridge. But these weren't to be. As *Rocket* and *Mallard* had excited past generations, so the tunnel has intrigued today's, and such an interest in trains couldn't have come at a better time for the railway.

All change

For some years it had been struggling with ever-increasing competition from both air and road transportation, but that was about to change.

Consisting of three tunnels (a rail tunnel each way and a central service tunnel) and measuring 31 miles long, with 23 of those under the seabed, the tunnel is an incredible feat of engineering. To get an idea of its size, take a look at the Channel Tunnel ring displayed in the Museum.

The idea of tunnelling under the English Channel was not a new one. It had been dreamt about since the mid eighteenth century, but it took until 1994, over 200 years and £8$\frac{1}{2}$ billion later, to become a reality.

During its construction, the French were also busy building a new high-speed rail link between Calais and Paris. The new track meant trains could reach speeds of 186 mph (300 kph) on that section of the journey – a speed England hopes to match in the near future.

Eurostar

Currently, the Eurostar train can travel from London Waterloo to Folkestone, through the tunnel to Calais and on to Paris in just three hours. Needless to say, the new route has been welcomed by freight

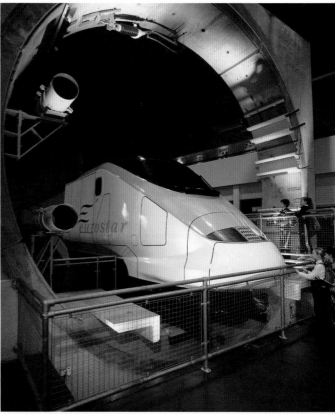

companies. By 1998 Railfreight Distribution was, on average, sending 20 trains a day through the tunnel to France and beyond.
In addition, regular shuttle trains ferry cars and lorries along the same journey.

Privatisation

Meanwhile in Britain, the Government had decided to return British Rail to private ownership with the passing of the Railways Act in 1993. Today's new train operating companies are run differently from those of the past in that they do not own any track, stations or signalling equipment. These all belong to a company called Railtrack. Nor do they own any locomotives or carriages. These are now provided by leasing companies. In fact, all that the operating companies actually own are time slots in which they can run trains. Perhaps the only similarity between today's private rail companies and those of the past is the riot of colour that decorates them.
The Museum's trackside viewing balcony allows you to see this for yourself on the East Coast Main Line.

Throughout Europe there is a new life and vigour about railways. Increasing freight traffic has brought new wagon-building business to York's former carriage works and faster electric trains are continually being developed to compete with cars and aircraft for travelling between major cities. France and Germany have both introduced high-speed train services that run on dedicated tracks. The ICE train in Germany, for example, reaches speeds of 175 mph (280 kph). Other countries have chosen to improve speeds on existing lines by introducing tilting trains like Sweden's X2000 and Italy's Pendolino.

In Britain, the Government is working towards an integrated transport policy. The plan is to improve interchanges and connections between rail services and between rail and other means of transport. This 'New Deal' for transport promises more through ticketing, better travel information, more reliable and flexible services and improved choice between different modes of transport.

Railtrack and the train operating companies are beginning to invest in a new round of improvements to trains and track which will see – on some routes at least – faster passenger trains and more capacity for freight.
Watch out for it.

RAILWAY GIANTS

Britain built an incredible 110,000 steam engines between 1804 and 1971, not to mention numerous electric and diesel locomotives as well.

Here we present some of the most famous in the National Collection. They are the ones that have touched the most hearts; they are the pride of the Museum; they are the 'Railway Giants'.

Stephenson's Rocket

First, in order of historical appearance, is *Rocket*. We keep the original at the Science Museum in London whilst at York we have a working replica, built in 1979 to celebrate the engine's 150th anniversary. *Rocket* is steamed regularly not only at the Museum but while on visits to exhibitions around the world.

Stirling Single

4-2-2 locomotive No.1 was the creation of Patrick Stirling – Chief Mechanical Engineer of the Great Northern Railway. Built in 1870 at Doncaster Works it was, as its number suggests, the first of 53 engines in this elegant design. Part of its appearance was down to Stirling's dislike of domes on locomotive boilers. He often designed engines without them – even though doing so made them harder to drive. But the huge driving wheels made his locomotives some of the fastest in the world and they regularly performed for the East Coast route during the famous 'Races to the North' between London and Scotland in 1888 and 1895.

The Chinese Locomotive

British manufacturers made locomotives for customers worldwide. In 1935 the Vulcan Foundry in Lancashire won a contract to supply 24 steam engines to the Chinese National Railways. Standing over 15 feet tall and more than 93 feet long, they were the largest single-unit locomotives ever built in this country. When the Chinese Government donated one to the Museum, its size meant that it couldn't travel here by rail. Instead it was delivered from Tilbury Docks by road, carefully avoiding low bridges along the way.

Ellerman Lines

One locomotive in the Museum that always attracts visitors is *Ellerman Lines*. This passenger engine worked for British Railways from 1949 to 1966. Its right-hand side has been cut away to reveal its internal construction and workings. Interestingly the three

elements that made *Rocket* so successful in 1829 (the multi-tube boiler, the blast pipe and the direct drive from the cylinder to wheels) were still being used 120 years later.

Another British Railways engine in the Museum is the mixed-traffic locomotive *Evening Star*. Built at Swindon Works in 1960, it was designed to haul both passenger and goods trains with equal ease. It was the last steam locomotive made for BR and to mark its place in history was painted as a passenger locomotive, given a copper-capped chimney and a plaque, proclaiming its status.

As steam trains began to disappear, inspiration for new locomotives came in the form of naval patrol boats – not as absurd as it sounds. Their light but powerful

'Deltic' two-stroke diesel engines could be adapted to enable locomotives to travel continuously at over 100 mph. The Deltic locomotives had arrived. Their power, speed and sound made them legends. From 1959, 22 of them were built and performed magnificently on the East Coast Main Line until the early 1980s when they were made redundant by an even better design. In semi-retirement, two Deltics often pull the luxurious Orient Express and are occasionally to be seen between journeys at the Museum, which is also home to the distinctive 1955 prototype.

The engine responsible for the demise of the Deltics was the aptly-named High Speed Train. Built in Crewe Works between 1976 and 1982,

HSTs, as they are commonly known, represented a departure from the traditional locomotive-hauled trains; they were complete ten-car sets with aerodynamically-shaped diesel-electric power cars at each end. The prototype alone, introduced in 1972, quickly set several

world speed records in the 140 mph range. The introduction of HSTs provided much needed improvement to the train service – without the need to rebuild, replace or even electrify the existing track and they remain the main-stays of several inter-city routes today.

MALLARD

Steaming into the history books at 126 mph.

NOT A DROP OF TEA SPILT

So read the *Daily Mail* headline on 4 July 1938.

But in reality *Mallard's* record-breaking run was no picnic. The train shook so violently that crockery smashed to the floor. And given the chance, the guard would have happily got off.

One man with no regrets however was Sir Nigel Gresley from the London & North Eastern Railway. He was the reason that everyone was there.

Gresley's inspiration

Four years earlier, inspired by the Bugatti railcars in France, he had started designing his own streamlined locomotives.

The first of the resulting A4 locomotives rolled out of Doncaster Works less than a year later. But the celebrations didn't last long.

In creating a new engine, Gresley had created a new problem. His faster train was now too quick for the old-style brakes.

So, in 1936 the Westinghouse Brake and Signal company got

a call. And two years later, an A4 locomotive named *Mallard* was chosen to help test a new quick service vacuum braking system.

To the limit

It was on one such test that Gresley saw the opportunity to push his train to the limit and win back the British speed record recently set at 114 mph by the rival London Midland & Scottish Railway. Perhaps they could even break the world record held by the Germans at 125 mph.

So on 3 July 1938, pulling six coaches and a dynamometer car for measuring speed and power, *Mallard* headed south from Grantham Station, bound for the record books.

Shattered

The driver, Joe Duddington, and his fireman, Tommy Bray, steadily built up the speed and it wasn't long before sleepy Little Bytham Station was rudely awoken as *Mallard* thundered through at 122 mph. Local tradition has it that coal flew from the engine's tender, showering the platforms and

smashing the station's windows as she passed.

But Joe needed to go faster. He'd soon have to slow down for the rapidly-approaching Essendine Junction. Throwing caution to the wind and muttering, 'Go on girl, you can do better than this,' he urged her on to 125 mph. With engineers praying in the back – not just for the record – *Mallard* finally reached 126 mph and held it for 306 yards before easing back for a more leisurely approach to Peterborough.

After her record-breaking run, *Mallard* was really put to work, hauling express trains on the East Coast Main Line and regularly pulling the Yorkshire Pullman between London, Doncaster and Leeds. She played her part in the Second World War too, moving men and materials for the war effort.

More recently, British Railways used her for the prestigious non-stop run between London and Edinburgh, until 1963 that is,

when she eventually retired from service having travelled almost 1½ million miles.

Today you'll find *Mallard* reunited with the dynamometer car and taking pride of place in the National Railway Museum.

She was restored to running order in 1988 to celebrate the 50th anniversary of her achievement. And to this day the record remains unbroken.

Sadly, *Mallard* is no longer able to steam, but who knows what's to come? After all, she's yet to have her 100th anniversary...

FLYING SCOTSMAN
A NON-STOP SUCCESS STORY

It was a locomotive designed specifically for long distance travel, but not even its creator could have known how far it would go. The year was 1923. The locomotive was *Flying Scotsman*.

Engineer, Nigel Gresley, built his Class A1 Gresley Pacifics in Doncaster for the sum of £7,944 each. *Flying Scotsman* was the third locomotive of this type.

Soon after her completion, *Flying Scotsman* was presented to the world at the British Empire Exhibition in London where she was admired by millions. Representing the latest in steam technology her appearance was so successful that she returned the following year.

'The Flying Scotsman' had been the name of the 10 o'clock express from London

Kings Cross to Edinburgh Waverley since 1862. So, when the very first non-stop luxury express service was introduced on 1 May 1928, it seemed only right that *Flying Scotsman* herself was chosen to lead the historic trip.

Final adjustments

At the time, it was to be the longest non-stop service in the world, stretching over 392 miles. Before such an epic trip was possible a specially

designed corridor tender had to be fitted to *Flying Scotsman* to allow her crew to change mid-journey. The first ever non-stop service successfully rolled into Waverley station in a record 8hrs 3min. (Forty years on *Flying Scotsman* beat her own record by completing the trip in 7hrs 36min!)

While travelling between Leeds and London six years later, *Flying Scotsman* received yet more acclaim by achieving

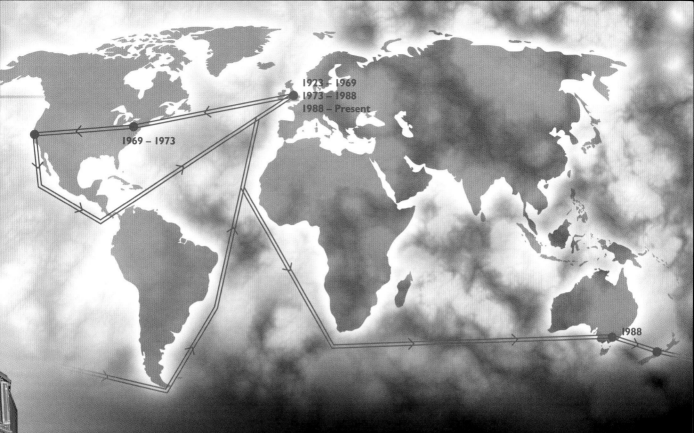

the first authenticated 100 mph for steam traction. A feat that secured her place in the history books for a second time.

Flying Scotsman continued normal duties throughout World War II and in 1947 was fitted with a new boiler and upgraded to an A3 class locomotive. It wasn't until 1963, having travelled some 2,076,000 miles up and down the UK, that Flying Scotsman finally retired. Seventy similar locomotives were scrapped to make room for the new generation of diesel locomotives. Thankfully, Flying Scotsman was saved from such a fate when rail enthusiast Alan Pegler purchased her for £3,000. The sole survivor of her class, she embarked on a programme of private main line excursions.

In 1969 following an offer to embark on a 2 year North American tour, she was shipped to Boston, USA. Extra equipment such as cowcatchers and an American bell were fitted to enable her to travel safely on US tracks. But Flying Scotsman's non-stop success was about to face its first red light. Back in Britain the political climate had changed causing many of the tours' sponsors to pull out. With no backing, the UK's most celebrated steam engine was left stranded in a US army base.

Salvation

Eventually in 1973 new owner, Sir William MacAlpine, arranged for her safe return to Britain. Having arrived home, her celebrity status was back on track. Between 1975-85 she toured the UK extensively where, as well as carriages, she would always pull large crowds. She even appeared alongside Dustin Hoffman and Vanessa Redgrave in the film 'Agatha'. Unfazed by her previous journey overseas, in 1988, Flying Scotsman embarked on a highly successful tour down-under to celebrate the Australian bicentennial. Whilst there she entered the history books once again by completing a record non-stop run by steam of 422 miles – the journey took 9hrs 25min and required 7 drivers!

She returned to England, but on 28 April 1995 was withdrawn from service a second time having suffered a cracked firebox. Southall Depot, where she lay in pieces, could easily have been her final destination. But in 1996 Dr Tony Marchington bought the engine for a staggering £1.5 million and embarked on a major restoration project.

No expense spared

Fully restored, she emerged from the West London depot to make her inaugural run from Kings Cross to York on 4 July 1999. Enthusiastic passengers paid £350 each to ride behind her. By now, Flying Scotsman had impressively spent more time in preservation than in actual service. And in April 2004, she was up for sale again. Fears of her being sold overseas provoked overwhelming public support for the National Railway Museum's bid to keep her in Britain. Finance came from far and wide: the National Heritage Memorial Fund put up a £1.8 million grant and the general public raised more than £3/4 million, including a donation of £365,000 by Sir Richard Branson. A further £500,000 from Yorkshire Forward, the Regional Development Agency for Yorkshire, helped ensure enough funds were available to keep the very best of British engineering running for many years to come.

FLYING SCOTSMAN IN PRINT

Our first poster (top left), dating from 1928, was produced by the LNER to advertise 'The Flying Scotsman', its principal express service between London King's Cross and Edinburgh Waverley. The poster highlighted the unique tenders fitted to locomotives on this service during summer months. The corridors which were incorporated into their design allowed train crews to

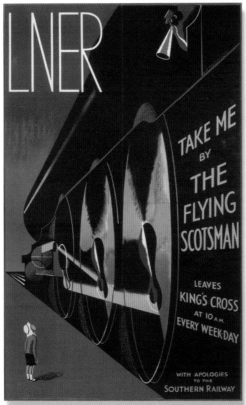

change over whilst on the move, making a non-stop service possible. Maurice Beck's 1932 poster highlights the 'Cocktail Bar', one of many high-class amenities provided on 'The Flying Scotsman'

service. Also dating from 1932, A.R. Thomson's poster grossly distorts the size of the *Flying Scotsman* locomotive to give the impression of speed and efficiency. The poster is a caricature of the Southern

Railway's famous 1924 'little boy' poster and powerfully makes the point that with *Flying Scotsman,* the LNER has the largest locomotives. The final poster dates from the 1950s and was produced by

British Railways to advertise 'The Flying Scotsman' weekday service. Its design was far more utilitarian than its predecessors with the times of the service just as important as the artwork itself.

LIVING
LEGENDS

Witnessing the unmistakable sounds, sights and smells of a steam locomotive can be an awesome experience. And it's for this reason that the National Railway Museum has made it policy to restore many of its engines to working order.

But there are exceptions. Exhibits like *The Agenoria* built in 1829 are far too old and fragile to be renovated while others, like the huge Chinese locomotive, are simply too big to run on British tracks. For engines like these the Museum really is the end of the line.

Where possible, however, and when external funding can be found, locomotives are returned to running condition. Much of the craftsmanship involved in doing this is undertaken in the Museum's workshops. Where possible, we give visitors the chance to see at first hand the work progressing on cylinders and frames and watch all the finishing touches being applied to the boilers.

Once a locomotive is working and has passed all the necessary safety checks, it is permitted to haul special steam trains on the main line. Perhaps the most spectacular of these runs is the Settle and Carlisle line which travels over the majestic Ribblehead Viaduct. Recently restored, the London & North Eastern Railway locomotive *Green Arrow* was photographed crossing Ribblehead.

The Duchess

Other Museum locomotives which have been seen on the main line include *Duchess of Hamilton* the *Stirling Single*, *Evening Star* the *Midland Compound* and the record-breaking *Mallard*.

Unfortunately, however much we enjoy seeing our trains working, while they're away, they obviously can't be viewed at the Museum. So a balance has to be struck between operating and displaying these preserved locomotives.

Some trains can be seen running at the Museum.

Replicas of older locomotives like *Rocket* and the broad gauge *Iron Duke* are steamed regularly on-site. The replicas look and indeed work like the original locomotives, the only difference being that they are made from modern materials and incorporate modern safety devices which allow them to haul short trains safely and give rides to Museum visitors. When aboard, you can almost imagine those pioneering days when *Rocket* stole headlines along with the nation's hearts.

In addition to its steam collection, the Museum also has several diesel locomotives in operating condition, all of which can be seen demonstrated at certain times throughout the year when visitors are invited to ride behind them.

The Museum has a narrow gauge track in its gardens, which is used by a variety of engines from time to time. There are two steam locomotives, *Taw*, a commercially-built model of a tank engine which once operated on the Lynton & Barnstaple Railway and *Margaret*, a model constructed in the Museum's workshops of a tank engine which used to operate in the Welsh slate quarries. The line is also the home of two petrol-driven diesel locomotive models, *John* and *Helen*.

Lending trains

The National Railway Museum loans some 30 locomotives to other Museums or preserved railways. This means that you'll often find our engines not only on the main line, but at places like the North Yorkshire Moors Railway, the Bluebell Railway in Sussex and the Great Central Railway at Loughborough. So, look out for them and enjoy the romance and splendour of steam and early diesel locomotives for yourself.

Although passenger travel wasn't the largest money earner for Britain's railways until the 1970s, opposing rail companies fought for it from the beginning, often going to remarkable lengths to portray themselves as offering the best service.

Competition

For rival trains running up the east and west coasts of Britain there was quite literally a race for supremacy. The most famous of these took place between London and Edinburgh in 1888 and London and Aberdeen in 1895. On leaving London, the trains would stop at nothing – including stations – to arrive first in Scotland. Timetables were ignored and trains shortened in an effort to improve speeds. The races eventually came to a climax in August 1895 when a West Coast train which had been hauled by a locomotive named *Hardwicke* – now on display in the Museum – completed the journey to Aberdeen in just 8 hours 32 minutes – a time only bettered 80 years later by the InterCity 125 trains.

But speed wasn't always an option. The Midland Railway's route to the north was a far more leisurely one. So, to attract their passengers they promised a luxurious journey. This they did in 1875 by abolishing second class travel, thereby bringing third class up to the standard of second. The Midland's third class dining car built in 1914, and on display in the Museum, is a good example of the quality they offered. It has wide, comfortable seats, mahogany veneered tables and silver-plated holders for wine bottles. Mind you for passengers able to afford first class, such comfort was nothing. They enjoyed the luxury of a Pullman.

First-class service

Introduced from the United States in the 1870s, Pullman coaches were the epitome of travelling in style. *Topaz*, in the Museum's collection, is typical of their opulence with its individual velvet armchairs, inlaid marquetry panels and bells to summon waiters should you desire a meal or drink brought to your seat. The *Golden Arrow* and the *Brighton Belle* were both Pullmans.

Another train renowned for its luxury is the *Flying Scotsman* – possibly the most famous express in the world. When the London & North Eastern Railway introduced this non-stop London to Edinburgh service in 1928, they provided everything from a hairdressing salon, a ladies' retiring room and a cocktail bar, to a restaurant car decorated in lavish Louis XVI style.

Specials

To some though, real grandeur meant having your own transport. Satisfying this market was left to 'Specials'.

THE GREAT AGE
OF
RAIL TRAVEL

Individuals or families could rent these trains for their exclusive use. Notably, Winston Churchill hired one for his 1910 election campaign and in August 1876, 17 tourists chartered one for a mystery tour of the British Isles. The really wealthy could go a step further.

The Duke of Sutherland, for example, actually owned his own carriage – which is now in the Museum. He had his own locomotive too, and if that weren't enough, his own private station near his home in Scotland.

Trains carried with them a sense of glamour, sadly long since lost in these days of tight timetables and busy tracks. However one train, above all, has immortalised the romance of rail travel. Since 1883, the Orient Express has connected Paris with the mysterious east. Originally supplied by the Compagnie Internationale des Wagons-Lits, the train was designed in a distinctive and opulent style.

Night Ferry

The same company produced carriages for the 1936 *Night Ferry* service which crossed the Channel to France. The blue and gold sleeping cars – an example of which is in the Museum – enabled travellers to go to bed in London and wake up in Paris thanks to a ferry specially-designed to carry the railway carriages.

These days, rail companies compete for supremacy in similar ways. Eurostar boasts of taking us to France or Belgium in three hours, a revitalised Orient Express continues to bring railway romance to life, and in Canada, the Canadian Pacific Railway has fitted its trains with special observation saloons to give wonderful views of the Rockies. But if it's sheer time on a train you're after, book a ticket on the Trans-Siberian Express. The journey takes a week and covers the 6000 miles from Moscow to Vladivostock. Needless to say it has a buffet car!

This is the Night Mail crossing the border,
Bringing the cheque and the postal order,
Letters for the rich, letters for the poor,
The shop at the corner, the girl next door...

W.H. Auden wrote this famous poem to accompany 'Night Mail', a short film celebrating the success of the Travelling Post Office. And a success it was. The Royal Mail was quick to recognise the potential of the railway. Just one year after Stephenson had won the Rainhill Trials, they were putting mail on trains travelling between Liverpool and Manchester.

Previously mail had always been transported by horse-drawn coaches, whose speed and efficiency had become legendary, but good as they were, they were no match for the power of steam. Trains could not only carry more mail, but could carry it at a far greater speed, providing a more efficient service.

The Travelling Post Office

By 1838, the mail was even being sorted on trains. At first these Travelling Post Offices – TPOs as they were known – were simply converted horseboxes, but as they became increasingly successful, special mail-sorting carriages were built. Included in the design was an ingenious bag and catching net to enable trains to collect and drop off mail en route, without having to stop.

But knowing when to have the heavy, leather bags ready for exchange was no easy task. TPO workers had to watch carefully for local landmarks along the route (usually at night!) and hang the bag out at just the right time. They were kept quite busy too, with up to 50 or 60 bag exchanges on one journey.

Harsh conditions

As with all new ideas, perfection was down to trial and error. At first, workers on board TPOs fell ill because of the constant shaking, the draughts from open doors necessary for exchanging bags of letters and from the fumes given off by the sealing wax used on the mailbags.

As a result, new coaches, like the 1883 West Coast Joint Stock TPO on show in the Museum, were built to improve working conditions.

Included in their design were thick mats to reduce vibration, seats for the sorters and all round better ventilation.

Auden

By the time Auden wrote his poem in 1936, there were 70 TPOs each day travelling the length and breadth of the country.

During the second half of the twentieth century however, as the Post Office introduced new systems, the number of

TPOs began to decline. But the mid 1990s saw mail-by-rail operations revolutionised with the introduction of new railway mail handling terminals at strategic centres such as London, Glasgow, Newcastle, Warrington, Doncaster, Bristol and Tonbridge. Nowadays the transfer of mail between road and rail happens with the minimum of delay and the familiar sight of mailbags being loaded on to passenger trains for distribution around the country has disappeared.

The Royal Mail even has its own electric trains to carry mail around the country – a cab from one of these modern units is on display in the Museum. Over 20 Travelling Post Offices still operate in Britain, but depending on where you live, your letters are just as likely to have been pre-sorted and placed in flat-pack containers ready for transfer between train, van or plane, thus providing us with the first-class service we receive today.

EGGS ↑↑↑ TO ELEPHANTS

For more than 100 years the railway was the only practical way to get goods of all kinds from the producer to the consumer.

Until 1962 rail companies were required by law to carry any load offered to them. At first however, coal and other minerals provided most of the traffic. Before long, industries were benefiting enormously by having their raw materials arrive at the factory quickly and their finished products delivered to market at a similar speed. As a result, major railway goods depots were built in all large towns and cities. Even smaller stations, at the very least, had a goods yard. The Museum's Station Hall was originally the goods depot through which much of the supplies to York's shops and factories arrived.

Rat-catchers

Railways also began to offer warehousing facilities at larger stations for commodities such as grain, cotton, wool and alcohol. The undercroft at St Pancras Station in London, for example, was used for the storage of beer from Burton-on-Trent. But these warehouses were not without problems; the railways were forced to employ rat-catchers to keep rodent infestation under control.

The sheer diversity of its cargo meant that the railway needed an equally diverse range of wagons. Minerals like coal would travel in open-topped wagons which were often owned by private businesses – there's an example in the Museum of one belonging to the Stanton Iron Company. Petroleum and other chemicals travelled in tankers, livestock were treated to wagons with the sides partially open for ventilation, chilled and frozen meats were carried in refrigerator vans cooled by ice, fresh meat was carried in ventilated vans with carcasses hung from hooks in the roof and bananas travelled in special steam-heated or heavily insulated vans – like the one in the Station Hall – to prevent frost damage in Britain's uncertain climate and to encourage ripening.

The sporting fraternity also required special vehicles to carry anything from horses to racing pigeons. Even entire circuses were moved by train.

Until the 1960s, freight traffic was the biggest money earner for the railway – shortly before the First World War, trains had been carrying over 500 million tonnes each year. But things were about to change. As the war in Europe came to an end and thousands of ex-army lorries started to be sold off by the Government, major competition from road haulage firms began to threaten the railway. So much so, that by 1938 the figure had dropped to just 263 million tonnes – 170 million tonnes of that being coal. Road haulage continued to increase throughout the 1960s and 1970s, reducing the railway's share of the freight market to less than 10 per cent.

Rising demand

Recently though, rail freight's future has started to look a little rosier with a wide range of materials once again being carried by rail, including, stone, scrap metal, coated pipes for the oil industry, motorcars, tanks, grain, potatoes, china clay, even domestic waste on its way to landfill sites.

The reasons for this revitalisation are not hard to find. New containers can now easily be unloaded on to ships and road transport; recent environmental concerns have led to grants to encourage investment; but perhaps most significant of all has been the steady rise of motorway congestion which has so often left road haulage at a standstill and cleared the way for businesses to return to rail.

STANTON

9988
TARE 7-4-3

Rocket

Mallard

Evening Star

Deltic

Stirling Single

The Bullet Train

Unmissable engines

Your journey through the National Railway Museum wouldn't be complete without seeing these magnificent locomotives at first hand.

Leaving
the tracks

Early railway owners had their fingers in many pies.

It seemed good business sense for those moving large numbers of people also to cater for them before and after their journey. Maybe they could supply a bus service taking passengers between stations and hotels? And if they did that, then why not own the hotels as well? The opportunities were endless.

Land

Realising this, rail companies began to build and buy hotels throughout the country, not just in cities, but at ferry ports as well. They even built hotels in golfing resorts like St Andrews, and in Turnberry and Gleneagles they actually built the golf course too. But they didn't stop at accommodation; they went on to command almost every form of transport imaginable.

Horses delivered goods by pulling carts from stations to nearby businesses. By 1913 the railway owned 26,000 of them and consequently needed stables and other facilities for their care. One such item, a horse ambulance, can be found in the Station Hall and was used to rescue 'broken-down' horses. Meanwhile, York's 100-horse railway stables lie adjacent to the Museum awaiting restoration.

Rail companies were continually looking for better alternatives to expensive horse power and in 1902 the Great Western Railway used a steam lorry to carry goods for the first time. Needless to say, most of the competition did the same shortly afterwards.

Soon, railway buses were introduced to feed people into the rail network. Railway-owned motor lorries and delivery vans travelled to and from stations and even household removals were organised.

By the time of nationalisation in 1948 the railways had around 13,000 road vehicles, although by 1980, after continually operating at a loss, these operations were largely abandoned.

Sea

The railway's involvement with ships started back in 1846. Over the years about 60 companies owned 1,250 vessels including tugs, dredgers, ferries and pleasure steamers. Models and paintings of some of these can be seen in the Museum.

By 1848, the railway had completed its first sea crossing with steamers running from Holyhead to Kingstown in Ireland. Other crossings quickly followed: Dover to Calais, Newhaven to Dieppe, Hull to Rotterdam and many more.

More often than not it was the railway company which developed the docks. The London & South Western Railway built Southampton docks, while the Manchester, Sheffield & Lincolnshire Railway bought the Grimsby Dock Company and completely modernised its facilities. They even opened a fish dock and sponsored deep-sea fishing.

Some companies though, were not content with extending existing docks. GWR, for example, built the harbour at Fishguard and the railway to it, in order to control one of the shortest crossings to Ireland.

And air

If ruling land and sea wasn't enough, a consortium of British railways launched air services in 1934 and played their part in the intensely competitive business – cut short by the war – of setting up a domestic airline network.

War also took its toll on the shipping operations. During the two World Wars railway ships suffered like others as a result of enemy action. The SS *Ouse*, for instance, a freighter run by the Lancashire & Yorkshire Railway, became one of 4,500 merchant vessels to be lost at sea when she was torpedoed in August 1940. Other railway company steamers were sunk as they assisted in the evacuation from Dunkirk.

By 1970, shipping had been separated from direct railway control into a new company called Sealink. Fourteen years later Sealink was sold, ending nearly 150 years of the railway at sea.

Today, most of the new train operating companies are part of larger groups with interests in buses, airlines and shipping. So perhaps the wheel has turned full circle.

ENGLAND'S LATEST PORT

IMMINGHAM *(Grimsby)*
DEEP WATER DOCK

COALING JETTY
WITH INDEPENDENT HOIST
FOR BUNKERING VESSELS
AT ANY STATE OF THE TIDE

For information apply to G. C. Goods Agents or Port Master, Immingham Dock, Grimsby. SAM FAY

A NEW OUTING!

DAY EXCURSIONS
BY
RAILWAY AIR SERVICES
FROM
SOUTHAMPTON

SPECIMEN FARES	
BRIGHTON	22/6
ISLE OF WIGHT	14/-
WESTON-SUPER-MARE	35/-
and many other places	

MULTI-ENGINED
AIR LINERS

Full particulars at your
local railway station.

ENGLAND'S LATEST SEASIDE HOTEL

MIDLAND HOTEL MORECAMBE
AN *LMS* HOTEL

LANCASHIRE & YORKSHIRE R?
EXPRESS TRAIN TRAFFIC COLLECTED
PARCELS AND LUGGAGE DELIVERED

Palaces on Wheels

When monarchs wished to tour their realm prior to the railway, it involved considerable effort. Travelling with them would be numerous household staff, wagonloads of luggage – including furniture – and a troop of mounted guards. Trips could take weeks.

The train was altogether more appealing. It not only cut journey times and enabled Kings and Queens to visit subjects who hadn't seen them before, but it was far more comfortable too. And comfort was of major importance.

A different class

Queen Adelaide – aunt to Queen Victoria, and widow of William IV – decided to use a train when visiting friends in the Midlands in 1840. The London & Birmingham Railway provided her with a personal carriage. The carriage, now on display in the Museum, included every conceivable luxury available, even a bed. Queen Adelaide's cousin – King Ernest Augustus of Hanover – was so impressed that he had an exact replica built for himself.

When Queen Victoria took her first ride by train in 1842, she too confessed to be "quite charmed by it"

particularly as it was "free from dust and crowd and heat". This pleased railway owners. They knew that as people saw their Queen travelling by train, those previously suspicious of its dangers would become intrigued. After all, if it's good enough for royalty...

Safety

As you would expect, everything was done to make the Queen's train as safe as possible. Crossings were guarded and a pilot engine would always travel ten minutes ahead of the royal train looking out for trouble. But danger was sometimes found elsewhere. When the Queen's driver was fatally struck by a low bridge in 1898, a train official chose to climb from a carriage, over the tender and drop into the driver's cab rather than disrupt her journey. It took something a lot more serious than a dead driver to stop the Queen's train.

Should Her Majesty want to go to bed on the other hand, well that's a different matter. Victoria refused to walk between coaches while the train was moving – a necessity until 1895 as the royal saloon comprised two carriages connected together.

As a result, officials were forced to bring the train to a complete stop until she was safely tucked in.

As new carriages were built, modern interiors and extras were always included. But later in her life Victoria became weary of such gadgets, refusing to use electric lights for example, although she soon warmed to the electric bell which proved so much more effective for summoning staff.

Following Queen Victoria's death, King Edward VII requested a new train to suit his own tastes. The carriages produced in 1902 for him and Queen Alexandra truly deserved the title 'Palaces on Wheels'. White enamel decorated the walls, giving the coach a spacious feel, while satinwood furniture inlaid with ivory ensured the royal family's comfort. Beautiful silver-plated baths were added to the bathrooms in 1915, although these were replaced in 1941 by the ceramic ones you can see in the carriages on display.

Down to earth

The coaches built for King George VI by the London Midland & Scottish Railway in 1941, although comfortable,

were far less grand. War had broken out in Europe and their design reflected it. Protective armour plating was fitted to the train and a more sombre external colour scheme reflected the needs of the times.

1977 saw the current royal saloons enter service and some of the wartime coaches enter the Museum. These new coaches were again less grand than earlier ones, looking more like hotel rooms than palaces.

Trains were never provided free of charge for the monarchy. They have always belonged to the railway companies and are in effect rented to the royal family when required. Bills were sent to the royal household for each journey and each passenger travelling – including the dogs.

The most recent change came in 1995, when two Class 47 locomotives were specifically assigned to pull the royal train. They were appropriately named *Prince William* and *Prince Henry*.

FIRM
but fair?

Life for early railway employees was full of ups and downs.

On the up side, they had a job for life – the railway wasn't about to disappear overnight. They received a free uniform – examples of which can be found in the Museum – travel concessions and they also benefited from cheap coal.

On the down side, hours were long and discipline harsh. Every employee, of which there were some 275,000 by 1873, had to know the company rule book and to regard it as a bible. One notable book – the North Eastern Railway's – contained such demands as 'Each man shall devote such time as may be required of him by the company's service' and 'he shall serve and reside where required'.

But it wasn't just the rules that were harsh; working conditions could be grim, especially in the early years.

The first locomotives had no cabs, which meant that the driver and his fireman were exposed to wind, rain and sometimes snow. Even the later engines often provided little shelter as you'll see from the *Stirling Single* in the Museum's Great Hall. If that weren't enough, the job itself was gruelling.

Hard labour

A fireman aboard a large locomotive, for example, would have to shovel a ton of coal every 40 miles; quite a feat. It was conditions like these, coupled with long hours and grievances over pay that sparked the growth of trade unions – but the railways were slow to recognise unions and it wasn't until the First World War that full representation was achieved.

However, despite the harsh working environment, employees considered it a privilege to be called a railway 'servant'. Besides, the railway companies weren't as unsympathetic as they may sound. For instance, the London & North Western Railway built houses, schools, parks and churches for their workers employed in Crewe, as did the Great Western Railway in Swindon.

Life on the railway

Such was the attraction of railway employment that boys of just 14 would start work as engine cleaners, with the hope that when they reached their mid-fifties, they'd have achieved the dizzy heights of express driver – experience, expertise and health permitting, of course. The medals and certificates that were often given to long-serving employees can be seen in the Museum.

Needless to say, such devotion to the railway was reflected in domestic life too; sons followed fathers into the service, daughters married railwaymen, wives operated crossing gates and strong rail communities were born.

Sports and social clubs flourished, and one in particular. A certain Premiership football team can trace its ancestry back to the Lancashire & Yorkshire Railway and the Newton Heath Locomotive Cricket and Athletic Club. Nowadays, its name is a little more snappy; Manchester United Football Club – no doubt the most famous 'railway' club in the world.

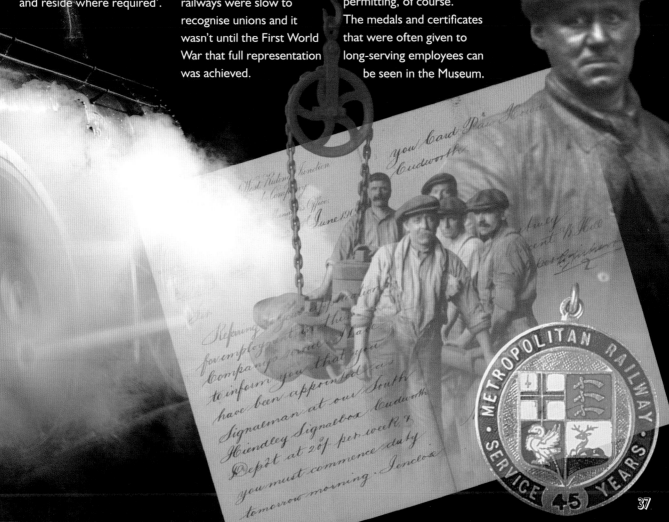

THE ART OF ADVERTISING

EAST COAST JOYS
travel by L·N·E·R
TO THE DRIER SIDE OF BRITAIN

EAST COAST JOYS
travel by L·N·E·R
TO THE DRIER SIDE OF BRITAIN

THE CENTRE FOR GLENEAGLES, TROSSACHS & ROB ROY COUNTRY.

BRIDGE OF ALLAN
STIRLINGSHIRE

GOLF, TENNIS, BOWLING, FISHING,
MINERAL WELLS.

An all the year round Health and Holiday Resort
CONVENIENTLY REACHED BY
THE CALEDONIAN RAILWAY

The pressure was on for rail companies. More and more lines were stretching throughout the country and with them came increased competition. Railways were going to have to work hard to sell themselves. But as they all offered pretty much the same thing, what they said and how they said it was critical.

For most of the nineteenth century, printed handbills were the main form of advertising. Early examples announcing services to markets and fairs have survived from around 1840. By the twentieth century however, a colourful revolution had taken place and the railways became lavish publishers of pictorial posters. Typically they invited people to travel – to restful holidays, to quiet waters or to a world of sunshine, sandy beaches and endless fun.

A new slant

In 1908 the designer John Hassall introduced the image of a carefree 'Jolly Fisherman' skipping along a beach. Albeit a slightly unconventional way to excite people about the joys of Skegness, his poster became so successful that it received long-lasting

recognition and was re-used many times. In fact, it's still in use today and by way of a tribute, a statue of the happy fellow stands proud in one of the local parks.

Natural beauty

But not all rail companies were so creative. Many believed that simply showing a beautiful illustration of a resort would be enough to entice people to travel there by train. The Caledonian Railway certainly thought so when it published a 1912 poster promoting the Bridge of Allan in Scotland.

Six in one

Advertising artists were always looking for new ways of selling rail travel. And in the 1930s, those promoting the London & North Eastern Railway had a stroke of genius. Realising that on larger stations there was often enough room to display more than one poster, they started designing sets of them; adverts that could be seen singly, but could also be put up side by side to create a continuous picture.

Tom Purvis was responsible for perhaps the most famous of these. His 1931 set titled

'East Coast' can be seen in the subway linking the Museum's Great Hall and Station Hall.

By the 1960s competition from cars, buses and even air travel was affecting the railways. Consequently their advertising shifted away from highlighting the resorts that could be reached by train – after all people would say, "that looks nice, let's jump in the car and go there". Instead railways started promoting themselves as being a better option than other forms of transport.

Carefree rail travel was frequently contrasted with hazardous car journeys, bedevilled by parking fines, speed traps and hold-ups. One TV advertisement featured travellers relaxing

on board an InterCity, playing chess, reading, kicking off their shoes and falling asleep. Even the chess pieces stretched and yawned before the strapline appeared: "Relax-InterCity."

The Museum is home to a huge amount of railway advertising. The collection is so vast that only a small part of it can be put on display. The rest is cared for in our library and can be seen by appointment.

Developing
Trains

With the invention of photography coming so soon after that of the steam railway, it's hardly surprising that the two complemented each other so often.

Since the 1840s many outstanding pictures have been taken of the railway at work and as a result, the Museum's library holds more than 1¼ million images which are regularly used by researchers and publishers.

Locomotives on their own, or pulling trains of various types, have always been a major focus for railway photographers. 'Steam up and waiting' was the title for this view of London & North Eastern Railway B1 Class locomotives at York Shed (in what is now the Museum car park) taken on 11 August 1947.

Cyril Herbert, *CCBH R24 31*

The sweeping curves and majestic arches of stations, bridges and viaducts provide inspiration for many photographers. The careful use of light together with an imaginative viewpoint can produce some truly stunning images.

John Click caught the early morning mist rising from the fields as a Class K3 2-6-0 locomotive headed north pulling a train of cattle vans on the former Great Central main line.

John Click, *Click 1/63*

The railway provided vital links to many of Britain's ports. This photograph of passengers disembarking on to a tender from the White Star liner SS *Cedric* was used to advertise the London & North Western Railway's links with transatlantic traffic. The photograph was taken at the LNWR's Holyhead harbour in 1909.

LNWR, *Euston photographer LMS 1880*

Photographers are drawn to the railway for many reasons. Some are concerned with the railway itself, the machines that run on it and its array of impressive buildings. Their purpose is to record images carefully of a locomotive's mechanical details or the architectural splendour of a station.

For others, the attraction is to add a certain something to the overall picture. In such photographs, the settings and lighting conditions are just as important as the train itself.

Here, British Railways Class 2 2-6-2 tank locomotive No. 82044 passes Grove Ferry on the Canterbury to Ramsgate line in 1956 as a family outing crosses the river Stour on the hand-hauled ferry.

P. Ransome-Wallis, *PRW 9510*

Occasionally photographers will go to incredible lengths to get exactly the shot they're after. In this view of the construction of the magnificent St Pancras Station roof structure taken in 1868, the photographer must have taken his life in his hands. The albumen print was made from a 12 x 10 inch wet collodion glass plate, which meant that the photographer would have had to sensitise the plate in a mobile dark room, then climb up the 100 ft scaffolding carrying his bulky camera and tripod and take the shot before the wet plate could dry. He'd finally have to return to ground level as quickly as possible and run into his darkroom to develop, fix and wash the negative. The result speaks for itself.

Commissioned photographer for Midland Railway, *St Pancras 280/8*

"My own view is that it is possibly too good for its purpose."

The Midland Grand

Leading architect Sir George Gilbert Scott was referring to the Midland Grand Hotel at St Pancras Station (1876) when he made this remark about a building that he had designed himself. But he could so easily have been talking about any number of railway structures.

Apart from the earthworks that thousands of miles of railways needed, the railway companies built countless viaducts, tunnels, bridges, workshops, homes, stations and hotels. And they frequently employed the country's best designers,

architects and engineers to help them. Isambard Kingdom Brunel was responsible for hundreds of miles of route. Undoubtedly his most famous structure was the Royal Albert Bridge, its elliptical tube spans standing majestically above the River Tamar linking Devon and Cornwall.

Perhaps Robert Stephenson's greatest achievement was the Britannia Bridge which linked Wales and Anglesey, whilst it was Benjamin Baker and John Fowler who jointly designed what is probably the most famous railway bridge in the world – the Forth Bridge. Stretching for over a mile, their masterpiece was also the first large bridge made entirely of steel.

Early railway companies continually strove to impress. Architects aimed to make stations worthy additions to towns and cities, while at the same time making a statement about the railway company.

Gateway to the north

The magnificent Doric Arch at Euston Station, designed by Philip Hardwick and built in 1838, proclaimed in no uncertain terms that the London & Birmingham Railway was the gateway to the north. Sadly the arch was demolished in the 1960s, but you can get an impression of its scale from the size of its central gates, which are now on display in the Museum. Similarly the classical station at Huddersfield, designed by

Shaping the landscape

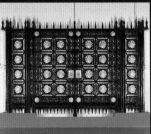

J.P. Pritchet Snr. celebrates the early railway's sense of triumph and achievement.

One of the hallmarks of the nineteenth century railway was the train shed. The design of these massive structures, frequently with innovative arched iron roofs, was both impressive and classically simple. The 700 ft long, 100 ft high and 240 ft wide example at St Pancras was, when built in 1868, the world's widest single span roof.

In the countryside, railways often used standard designs for their stations, partly for economic reasons but also to promote a corporate image. The London, Brighton & South Coast Railway chose two-storey Italian-style villas, the Great Western Railway built a miniature château at Slough and the Furness

Railway opted for Swiss chalet-type buildings.

Since the 1950s, many older stations have been redeveloped. Birmingham New Street, for example, was rebuilt in 1967 to become a purely functional structure beneath a shopping centre. More recently, a resurgence in station design at, for instance, Ashford and Waterloo International has seen innovative use of steel and glass in a distinctive post-modern style.

Carmichael's landscape

Since the very beginning, the impact of the railway on the landscape attracted the attention of artists. Viaducts, in particular, carried with them such presence that nineteenth century painters like T.T. Bury and John Wilson Carmichael found them

hard to ignore – examples of their work can be seen in the Museum.

Railway architecture has produced some of the Victorian era's greatest monuments and many buildings, like the St Pancras Hotel, are listed. The Forth Bridge is one of several railway structures being considered for World Heritage Site status.

Organisations like the Railway Heritage Trust work to conserve such architecture throughout the country. Wemyss Bay Station in Scotland has recently been restored with their help. Other listed sites have been imaginatively transformed, like the old signal box on York Station which has been turned into offices and a bookstall.

MAKING A NAME FOR THEMSELVES

Take away the paint, the lettering and the company emblem and, let's face it, for many people, one carriage looks much the same as another.

Early railway owners were quick to realise that it was essential for them to have a corporate identity which distinguished them from their competitors.

Branding the railway

With this in mind, they stamped their insignias on to every part of their business. Their logo appeared on cutlery, glasses, bedding, timetables, stationery, fire buckets, tickets, uniforms, the many hotels and stations owned by the railway, the porters' trolleys – even chamber pots proudly carried the company's crests.

Graphics ranged from simple initials to a full armorial coat of arms. Often the inspiration for the latter came from the main towns served by the line. Symbols like the knot of the North Staffordshire Railway became universally recognised.

They were particularly useful for the many workers who could not read.

Locomotives were distinguishable by their variety of colours, ranging from red, blue, black and yellow, to the most common of all, green. William Stroudley, who was responsible for the London Brighton & South Coast Railway's locomotives, was one such person to choose green. Unfortunately, Stroudley seemed to have suffered from colour blindness, as his shade of green, which he called "improved engine green", was in fact a kind of toffee brown. Perhaps no one dared tell him! *Gladstone* and *Boxhill*, two of his locomotives, can be seen in the Museum.

An eye for detail

When it came to actually painting engines, many companies took the most painstaking care. Each company had very specific methods of application. Paint was usually mixed in the railway's workshops to their own recipe, and, as there was no gloss paint available until the twentieth century, everything was painted in a matt colour and then given a generous coat of varnish.

In 1899 the Midland Railway produced the following specification for painting their locomotives:

"The boiler to receive two coats of lead paint before being lagged. The lagging of boiler and other parts to have one of lead paint then to be well-stopped and filled up properly, and rubbed down; then two coats of Oxide of Iron and sandpapered; then one coat of Oxide of Iron and Lake picked out with black and fine lined with yellow, then three coats of varnish". 'Lake' was crimson lake: you can see this rich red colour on two Midland Railway engines in the Museum.

Silver service

Despite differences in appearance, rail companies did tend to agree on one thing; only the best was good enough. Well-known manufacturers like Mappin and Webb would supply silver-plated ware for hotels and restaurant cars and china was supplied by Minton or Spode. In fact Minton supplied the crockery when the London & North Eastern Railway introduced their high speed *Coronation* train in 1937. The cutlery was specially commissioned to have flat handles, so as not to roll or rattle while the train thundered along. The glasses were supplied by the Edinburgh Crystal Glass Company and everything was decorated, of course, with the company's 'high-speed' logo.

So important was image that in 1932 LNER employed the leading graphic designer Eric Gill to advise on the introduction of his 'Gill Sans' lettering on all of their vehicles, station name boards, direction signs and, well, pretty much everything else. Look out for his *Flying Scotsman* headboard in The Warehouse.

The railways' habit of marking everything has encouraged a large collectors' market over recent years. Signals, lamps, tickets, notices, maps, cutlery and crockery are all in big demand from an array of private collectors, not to mention preserved railways and museums. In fact, such was the demand that British Rail actually opened a second-hand shop to sell all its out of date items. Thankfully, they didn't include their sausage rolls.

If you heard today that a new form of public transport could take you from England to Australia in a couple of hours, you'd no doubt be excited. And rightly so.

The arrival of the train was, in the nineteenth century at least, on a par. The benefit of improved transit for freight and passengers was such that within 20 years of the opening of the Liverpool & Manchester Railway the rail network had stretched throughout the country.

Charles Dickens summed up the railway's domination perfectly:

"There were railway hotels, office houses, lodging houses, boarding houses; railway plans, maps, views, wrappers, bottles, sandwich boxes and timetables.....there was even railway time observed in clocks, as if the sun itself had given in."

The railway time he spoke of is better known today as Greenwich Mean Time.

Previously, as travelling was so much slower, it didn't matter if, for example, Bristol followed a slightly different time from London. By the time you got there, a few minutes or even a quarter of an hour was neither here nor there.

Changing times

The speed of the railway changed all that. Having a standard and accurate time was essential for the smooth running of trains, so much so that all guards were issued with watches and large public clocks were displayed in stations. Some of these are now on show in the Museum, like the Euston Station clock – one of the first used to set railway time.

Day trippers

As travelling times fell, demand for travel grew. Where previously trips would have been unthinkable because of the time, cost and upheaval involved, now there was an explosion of people wanting to go to new places. Fast, cheap travel meant that a national football league became possible for both players and spectators. Horse racing too could take on a national dimension. And it wasn't long before the railway was taking millions to the seaside for the very first time.

In 1844, railway excursions were described as "the chief national amusement", and the following year a gentleman named Thomas Cook organised a "package tour" involving a train from Leicester to Liverpool. He never looked back.

The speed of the railway was not only beneficial to those who travelled on it. Short journey times meant that fresh food could now be distributed around the country at a much lower price. As a result, more people had access to fruit, milk and fish and the nation's diet improved. In fact, the railway was responsible for the birth of that most famous of British institutions, the fish and chip shop.

The ever-increasing number of lines also meant that people could live away from their place of work. Mill owners from Leeds and Bradford could live in Harrogate and, likewise, London bankers could travel from Brighton or Southend every day. Needless to say, growing numbers of people chose to commute, particularly in the South East, which often resulted in crowded carriages with standing room only.

As suburban lines became electrified, carriages were designed with this new 'rush hour' in mind. The Museum's London & North Western Railway electric motor coach of 1916, was built with plenty of space for 'strap-hanging', something we're all familiar with these days. Still, such discomfort on the way to work was considered a small price to pay to escape the overcrowded cities. Almost overnight it seemed that Britain had become a much smaller place.

A smaller Britain

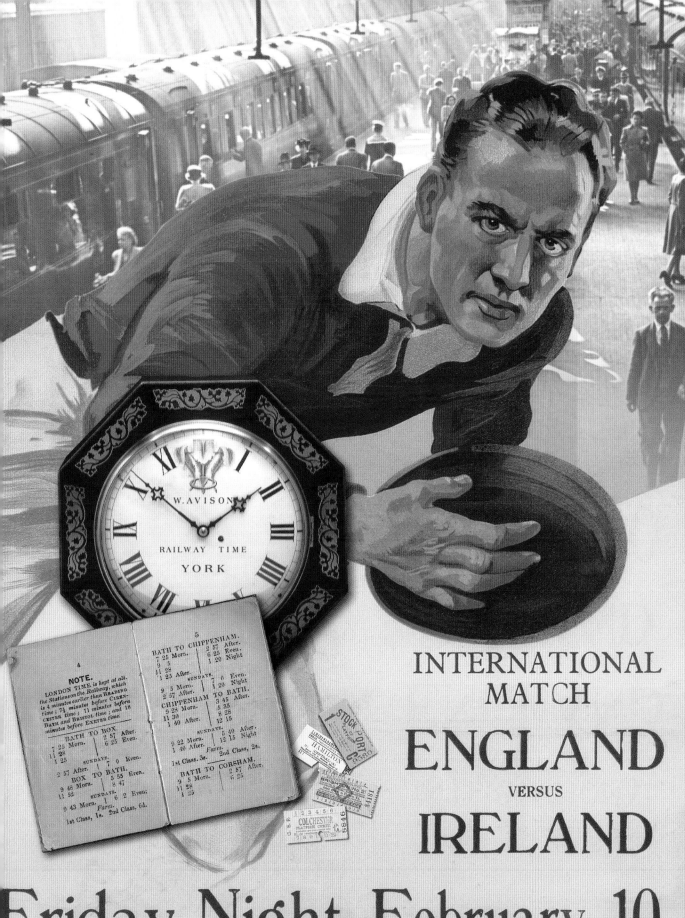

INTERNATIONAL
MATCH

ENGLAND

VERSUS

IRELAND

Friday Night, February 10

DAY EXCURSION TICKETS

Talking "Trains"

We've all 'let off steam', been 'on the right track' and 'seen the light at the end of the tunnel' at one time or another. We probably didn't give any thought as to the origin of these phrases, which shows just how much the language of trains has entered our popular culture.

Among the first to highlight the railway's influence was Charles Dickens. Impressed by both the size and power of this new form of transport, he described the construction of the first main line from Euston in the mid 1830s in his novel 'Dombey and Son'.

By the end of the nineteenth century, the railway had become a part of everyday life. It was no longer just being described in books but was part of the story itself. Conan Doyle would frequently have Sherlock Holmes and Dr Watson discuss their latest case aboard a train. And in 1898 H.G. Wells used the comings and goings at Woking Junction to set a scene of normality, prior to the dreadful events that were to unfold in 'The War of the Worlds'.

In a far less menacing way, children's literature began to involve the railway too. In E. Nesbit's 1906 book 'The Railway Children', the storyline itself revolved around trains, tracks and the local station.

Famous characters like Rupert Bear and Toad of Toad Hall began to use the railway as a means of going to exciting places or to have adventures. Inevitably, trains became famous characters themselves. Who hasn't watched or read a story involving Thomas the Tank Engine, a character who appears regularly at the Museum to the delight of thousands of visitors? Whole generations have gone to sleep dreaming of this loveable talking engine.

Lights, camera, traction

Of course authors weren't alone in recognising the increasing significance of the railway. The cinema used trains from the very start. In 1895 the Lumière brothers showed scenes of a train coming into a station, in what was one of the first demonstrations of moving pictures. In 1903, the first box office success, in fact, one of the first films to tell a story – 'The Great Train Robbery' – couldn't have involved railways more. Who doesn't recall the infamous scenario of the heroine tied to a track, only to be rescued from certain doom at the very last second?

Trains, it was discovered, could set the scene for any emotion. James Bond found both romance and danger on them, Agatha Christie wrote of murders aboard them, 'Schindler's List' used them to recreate painfully the horror of war as they carried Jews to Nazi concentration camps and what cowboy film was complete without a fight on top of a moving train?

Train journeys mean meetings and separations, so romance and the railways have inevitably become linked. Scenes of tearful farewells are engraved on everybody's mind. 'Brief Encounter', the classic love story set in a station buffet became perhaps the definitive British film for the wartime generation.

Our Halls of Fame

Film producers working on non-contemporary storylines often come to places like the National Railway Museum to find their stars. Several of the Museum's locomotives and carriages have appeared alongside famous actors in films like 'Chariots of Fire' (South Eastern & Chatham Railway locomotive No. 737 with Ben Cross and Alice Krige), 'The Dresser' (London Midland & Scottish locomotive *Duchess of Hamilton* with Tom Courtenay and Albert Finney) and 'Shadowlands' (Great Western Railway buffet car No. 9631 with Anthony Hopkins and Debra Winger). Railways even feature in TV advertisements for banks and telephone directories. In fact, the Museum's working replica of *Rocket* starred in a recent television advert for beer.

The railway has steadily become a part of all our lives, from the way we talk to the things we watch. And doubtlessly it will do so for many years to come.

THE FRONT LINES

In order to wage war effectively, armies require continual deliveries of supplies and regular reinforcements. The railway, it soon became clear, had the ability to provide both.

Its value first became apparent in 1842 when the Government ordered rail companies to transport hundreds of soldiers to Manchester in order to quell the Chartist riots that were taking place there.

But it was when war broke out overseas that the railways' full potential was realised. During the Crimean War a seven-mile stretch of track was laid from the harbour at Balaclava specifically to supply the front line at Sebastopol. And later, in the South African War of 1899-1902, the London & South Western Railway carried thousands of men and horses to Southampton Docks; a journey that continued to be made throughout the First World War when the port became a main embarkation point for millions of soldiers heading for the Western Front.

Useful allies

The role of railways soon became crucial to military planning. Consequently, at the start of the First World War the Government took control of all Britain's railways in order to give maximum priority to the war effort. Huge numbers of men and equipment were carried. Vast quantities of coal were transported to the northern tip of Scotland to fuel the Grand Fleet at Scapa Flow. A special Railway Operating Division was even set up in France specifically to serve the Front Line, taking fresh supplies in and wounded troops back to 'good old Blighty' in specially-equipped ambulance trains.

After the railways' heavy involvement in the First World War, it seemed only fitting that when the armistice was eventually signed, it was done so in a railway carriage – a fact not forgotten by Hitler, who demanded that the same vehicle be used 22 years later to accept the surrender of France.

World War Two

As war broke out for the second time, an even greater strain was put on the railways. Thousands of children had to be evacuated from major cities to 'safe' areas. As fighting continued, trains and lines became obvious targets for bombers and suffered enormous damage during The Blitz. In the Museum's Great Hall, a plaque in front of the sectioned locomotive marks the spot where one such bomb fell in April 1942.

But despite such a heavy aerial bombardment, the railways continued to move enormous numbers of goods and people. Passenger traffic had a lower priority than

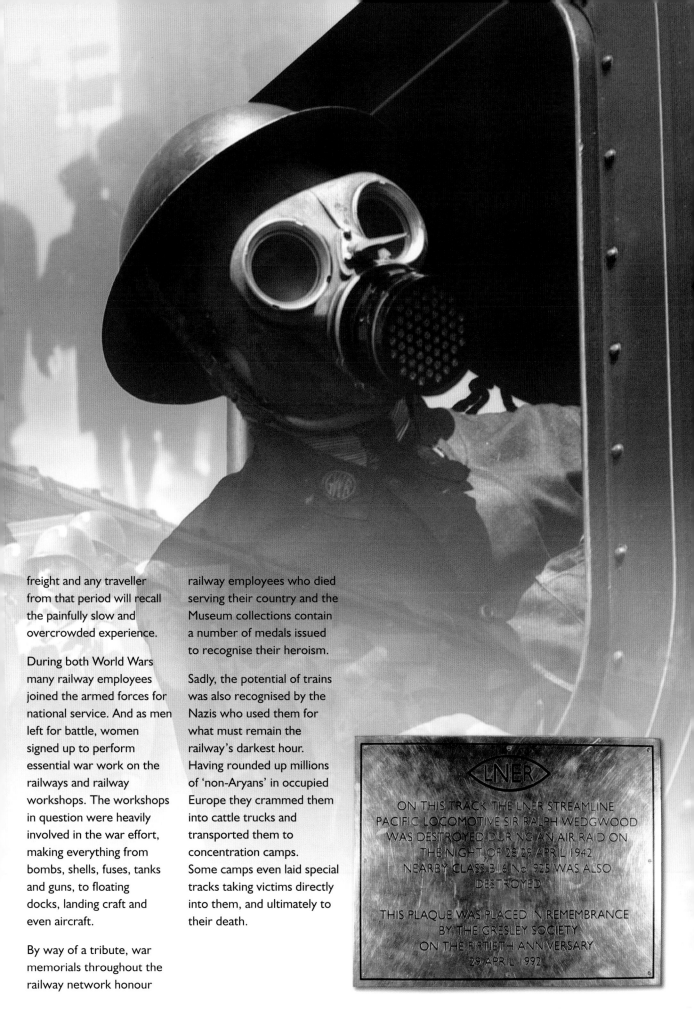

freight and any traveller from that period will recall the painfully slow and overcrowded experience.

During both World Wars many railway employees joined the armed forces for national service. And as men left for battle, women signed up to perform essential war work on the railways and railway workshops. The workshops in question were heavily involved in the war effort, making everything from bombs, shells, fuses, tanks and guns, to floating docks, landing craft and even aircraft.

By way of a tribute, war memorials throughout the railway network honour railway employees who died serving their country and the Museum collections contain a number of medals issued to recognise their heroism.

Sadly, the potential of trains was also recognised by the Nazis who used them for what must remain the railway's darkest hour. Having rounded up millions of 'non-Aryans' in occupied Europe they crammed them into cattle trucks and transported them to concentration camps. Some camps even laid special tracks taking victims directly into them, and ultimately to their death.

LNER

ON THIS TRACK THE LNER STREAMLINE PACIFIC LOCOMOTIVE SIR RALPH WEDGWOOD WAS DESTROYED DURING AN AIR RAID ON THE NIGHT OF 28/29 APRIL 1942 NEARBY CLASS B16 No. 925 WAS ALSO DESTROYED

THIS PLAQUE WAS PLACED IN REMEMBRANCE BY THE GRESLEY SOCIETY ON THE FIFTIETH ANNIVERSARY 29 APRIL 1992

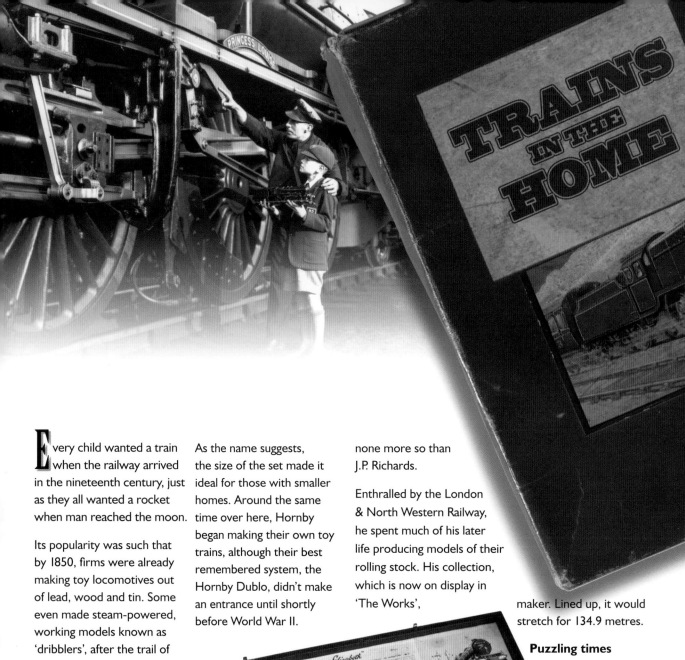

Every child wanted a train when the railway arrived in the nineteenth century, just as they all wanted a rocket when man reached the moon.

Its popularity was such that by 1850, firms were already making toy locomotives out of lead, wood and tin. Some even made steam-powered, working models known as 'dribblers', after the trail of water the engines left in their wake.

In 1891 the German manufacturer Märklin caused great excitement in the toy industry when it introduced model trains which ran on a figure-of-eight shaped track rather than just on the floor. This new train 'set' idea was to take the toy world by storm.

Set for success

In the 1920s another German firm – Bing – took the idea further with a 'Tabletop' version.

As the name suggests, the size of the set made it ideal for those with smaller homes. Around the same time over here, Hornby began making their own toy trains, although their best remembered system, the Hornby Dublo, didn't make an entrance until shortly before World War II.

Examples of various models have since taken their place in the Museum's collection.

But not all model trains are toys; amateur model makers have been fascinated by the railway since it began;

none more so than J.P. Richards.

Enthralled by the London & North Western Railway, he spent much of his later life producing models of their rolling stock. His collection, which is now on display in 'The Works',

consists of 150 coaches, 45 locomotives and a remarkable 450 wagons, each built to a precise 7mm scale and as accurate in detail as they could possibly be. The collection is perhaps the greatest ever produced to this quality by a single model maker. Lined up, it would stretch for 134.9 metres.

Puzzling times

Jigsaw puzzles, or dissected puzzles as they were first known, frequently featured pictures of locomotives and were often used to promote rail services. The earliest in the Museum's possession dates back to 1860, and shows the 'London Birmingham Liverpool and Manchester Railway' with pictures on both sides. On one is a railway map and on the other, a picture of their locomotives and carriages. But it was the Great Western

Railway which was perhaps the most prolific publisher of jigsaws. Between 1924 and 1937 they issued 43 puzzles. Such was their popularity, people would write to GWR to tell them how quickly they could complete them. In case you're wondering, the record appears to have been 15 minutes.

Suitable for all ages

Board games with railway themes were also popular. One of the earliest, produced in 1839, introduced the perils and pleasures of railway travel. Players would be fined for smoking on non-smoking squares and for being drunk on the journey. Needless to say, this particular game was geared more towards an adult audience.

Monopoly too, perhaps the most famous board game in the world, includes railway stations among the property to be bought and sold. And even Snakes and Ladders didn't escape the railway's influence. A special version of the game was produced in 1935. Should you be caught without a ticket or lose your luggage, you would slide down a snake and if you were fortunate enough to board an express, you'd go up a ladder. Nothing, it seemed, was untouched by the railway.

Even today the fascination with railway games continues, although now you're more likely to drive a train courtesy of your personal computer, or join the anarchic fun of Mornington Crescent on the Internet – a game inspired by a popular radio programme and based around a station on London Underground's Northern Line.

Museum map and services

The National Railway Museum is the largest of its kind in the world.

The collections in the Museum are vast, ranging from an Aladdin's Cave of objects in The Warehouse and a superb collection of Royal carriages in the Station Hall, to the giant locomotives of steam such as *Mallard* in the Great Hall. The exhibits you see today are only part of the National Railway Collection, as the Museum is responsible for far more objects than can be displayed.

Reference Library

The Museum has an extensive collection of books, archives, photographs, pictorial works and posters. The reading room is open free of charge from Monday to Friday from 10.00-17.00 (except public holidays). Please telephone: 01904 686235 to make an appointment.

Education Service

The Museum provides a wide range of services for visiting education groups of all ages. Teacher's Activity Guides, including worksheets for school parties, are available on request and groups are able to pre-book the Museum's Interactive Learning Centre for children. For further information please contact the Education Department at the Museum on 01904 686230.

Corporate Hire

It's not only school parties that come here. Our extensive facilities provide a unique setting for corporate hospitality, business meetings, private viewings, product launches, special celebrations and weddings. We have meeting facilities for 10 to 120 delegates and can cater for parties and dinners from 30 to 500.

Refreshments

Our licensed restaurant, *Brief Encounter*, is open daily and serves full meals or light snacks. During the summer, there is also a barbecue – weather permitting. And finally, throughout the holiday season our *Whistle Stop* café is open for light lunches and refreshments.

Gift Shop

You can find an array of souvenirs, presents, videos and books in our shop or you can phone for a mail order catalogue.

Facilities for visitors with disabilities

Ramps and lifts provide access to most parts of the Museum, automatic doors have been installed at both entrances and special parking is available at the City Entrance. Wheelchairs are also available.

Car Park

Long-stay parking is available on-site, for which a small charge is made.

Friends of the National Railway Museum

The Friends of the National Railway Museum support the work of the Museum. For further details please write to the Friends' Secretary at the Museum or telephone: 01904 636874.

Opening Times

Daily 10.00 - 18.00.
Closed 24 - 26 December.
For further information please contact:

The National Railway Museum
Leeman Road
York
YO26 4XJ

Telephone: 01904 621261.
Facsimile: 01904 611112.

e-mail:
nrm@nmsi.ac.uk

Web site:
http://www.nrm.org.uk